The Joy of Dancing Through the Ages

From Minuet To Rock

Selected and edited by Denes Agay

Yorktown Music Press, Inc.
New York/London/Paris/Sydney/Copenhagen/Berlin/Tokyo/Madrid

Cover illustration by Janice Fried
Project Editor: Felipe Orozco

Order No. YK 21967
International Standard Book Number: 0.8256.8112.X

Exclusive Distributors:
Music Sales Corporation
257 Park Avenue South, New York, NY 10010 USA
Music Sales Limited
8/9 Frith Street, London W1D 3JB England
Music Sales Pty. Limited
120 Rothschild Street, Rosebery, Sydney, NSW 2018, Australia

Printed in the United States of America by
Vicks Lithograph and Printing Corporation

Table of Contents

Minuet

Ludwig van Beethoven
(1770–1827)

TRIO

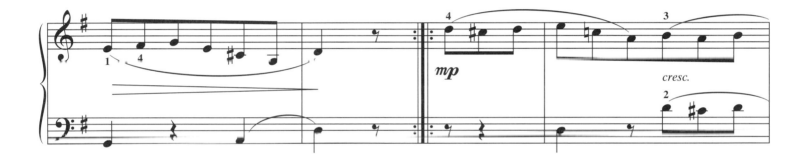

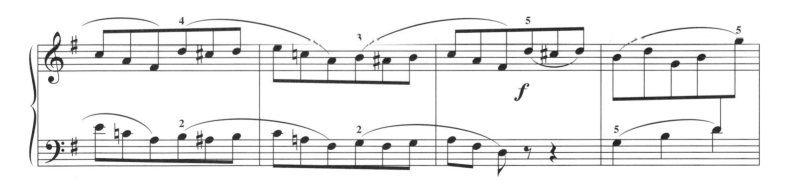

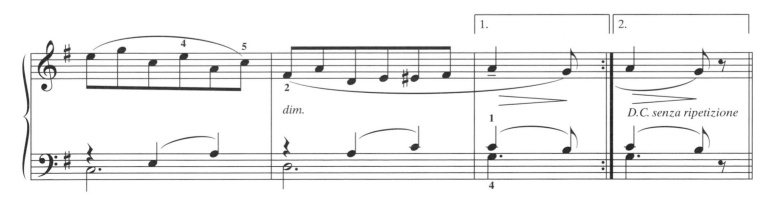

Minuet

Luigi Boccherini
(1743–1805)

Gavotte

Johann Sebastian Bach
(1685-1750)

Graceful walking tempo

Three Ecossaises

Ludwig van Beethoven
(1770–1827)

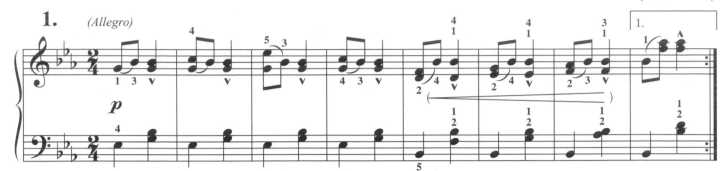

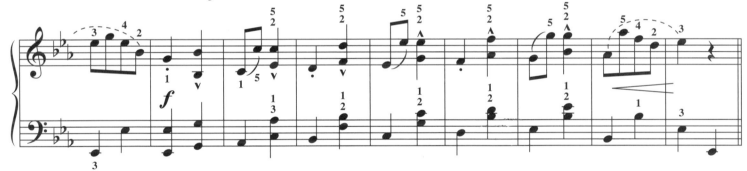

3. *(Tranquillo)*

Two Ländler

Franz Schubert
(1797–1828)

1. **Allegretto**

2.

Polonaise

Michael K. Oginski
(1765–1833)

Moderato, molto cantabile (♩ = 66)

Trio

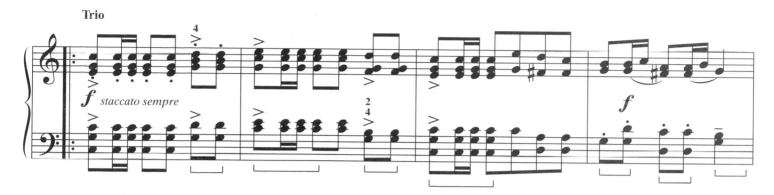

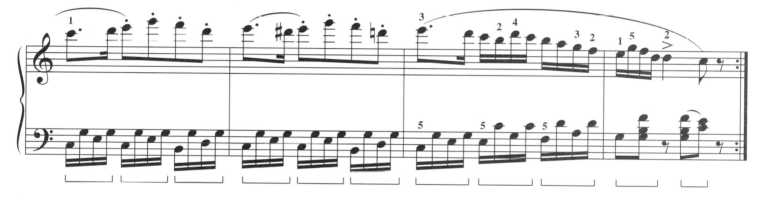

Mazurka

Frédéric Chopin
(1810–1849)

Polonaise Militaire

Frédéric Chopin
(1810–1849)

Lively, with spirit

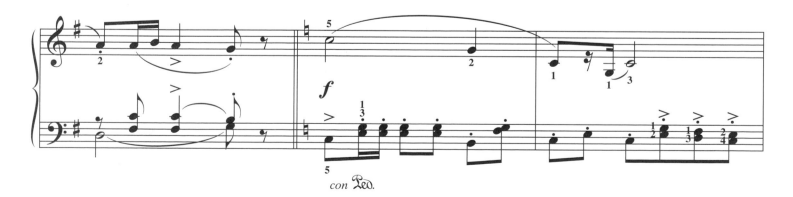

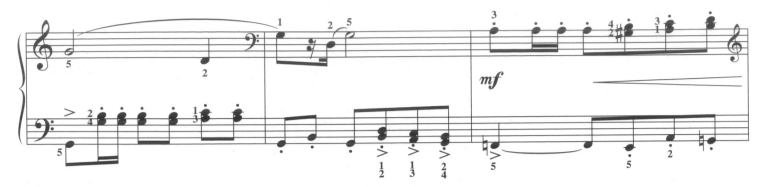

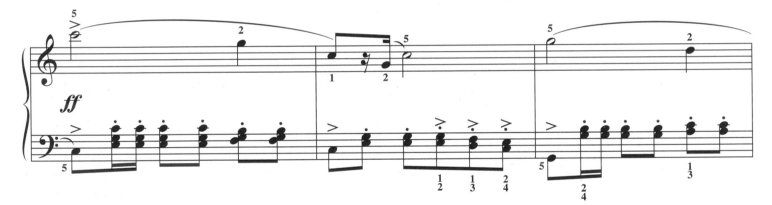

da Capo al fine
without repeats

Fine

Tarantella
(La Danza)

Gioacchino Rossini
(1792–1868)

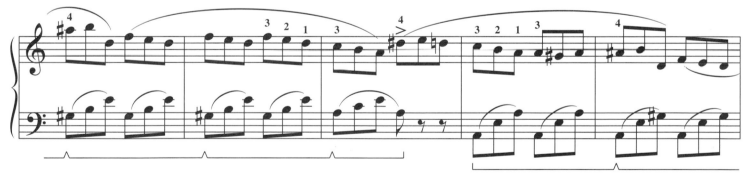

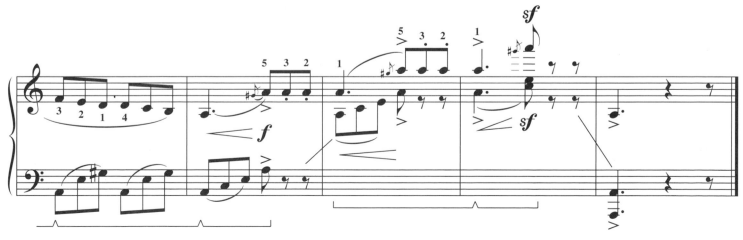

Csárdás
(Hungarian Folk Dance)

Traditional

Moderato with a strong beat

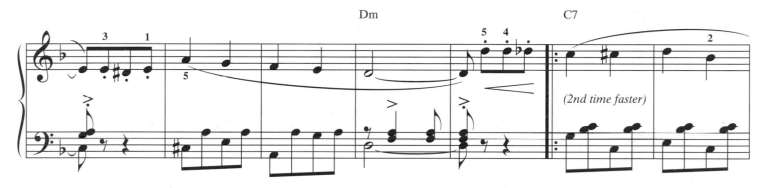

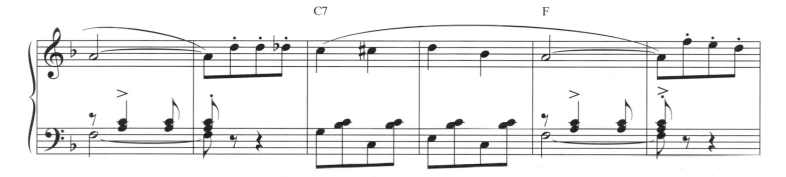

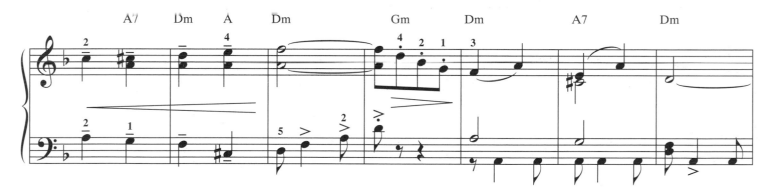

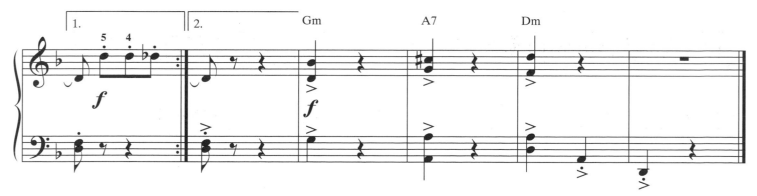

The "Fledermaus" Polka

Johann Strauss II
(1825–1899)

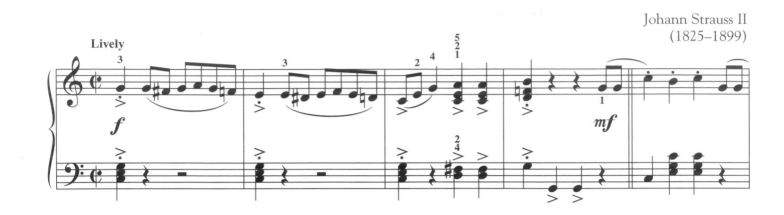

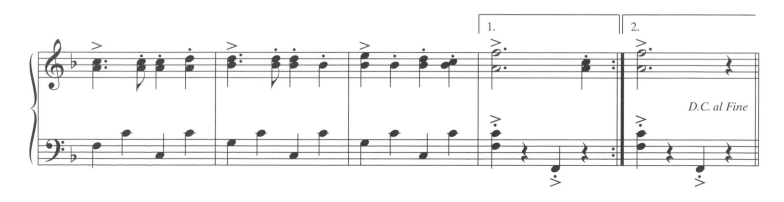

Waltzes by Strauss

"The Emperor Waltz"

Johann Strauss II
(1825–1899)

Moderately

"Wine, Women, and Song"

Slavonic Dance No. 8

Antonín Dvořák
(1841–1904)

Allegro molto

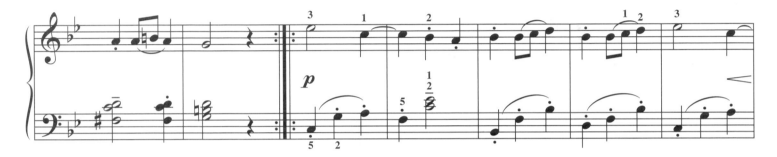

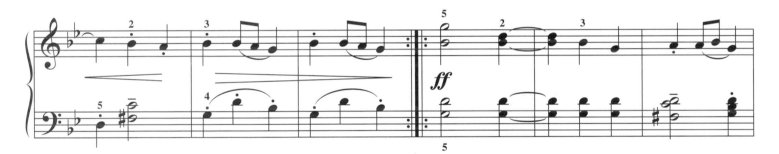

Presto

Can-Can
From the Operetta "La Vie Parisienne"

Jacques Offenbach
(1819–1880)

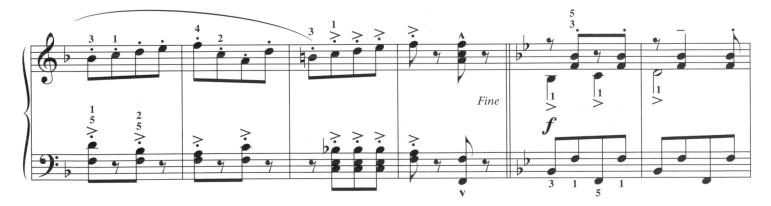

D.C. al Fine

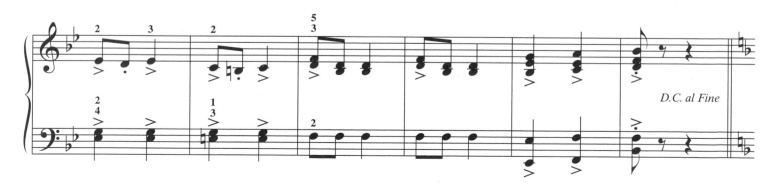

Valse Lente
From Coppelia

Léo Delibes
(1836–1891)

Spanish Dance
Playera-Andaluza (Danza Española Nº5)

Enrique Granados
(1867–1916)

Allegretto

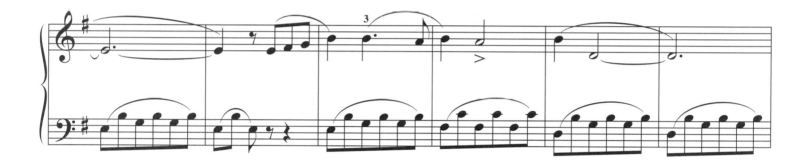

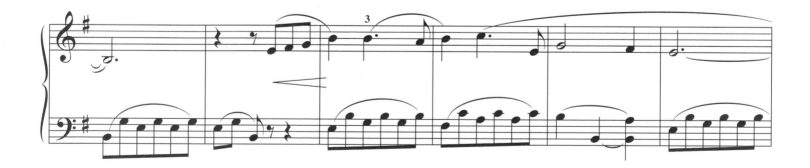

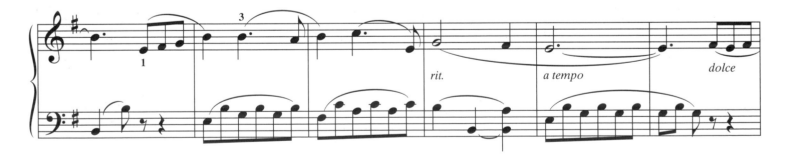

to Coda ⊕

Andante

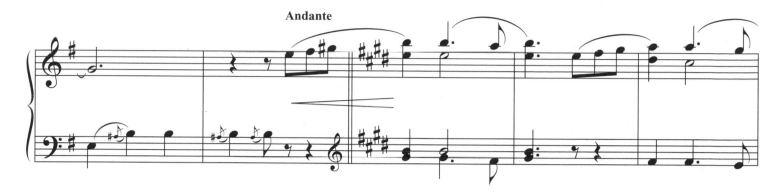

Tempo I

Coda

Cake-Walk

Kerry Mills
(1869–1948)

Lively, with very marked rhythm throughout

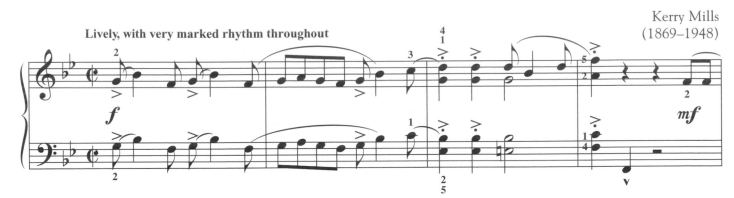

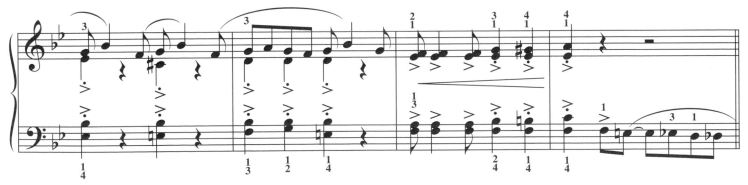

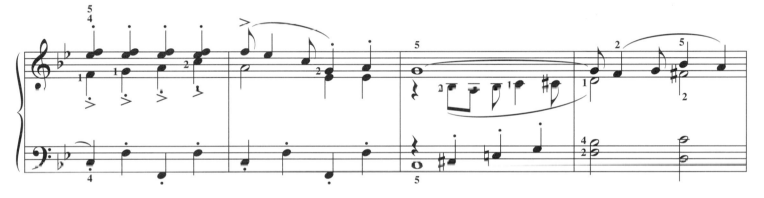

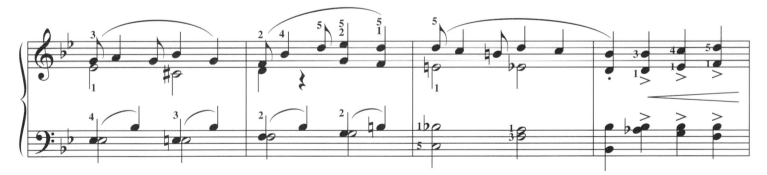

The Entertainer
Ragtime Two Step

Scott Joplin
(1868-1917)

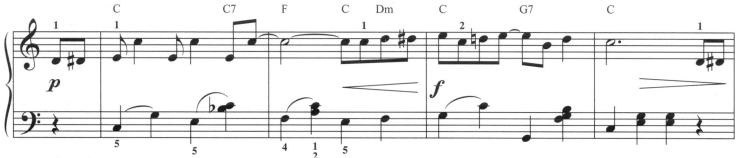

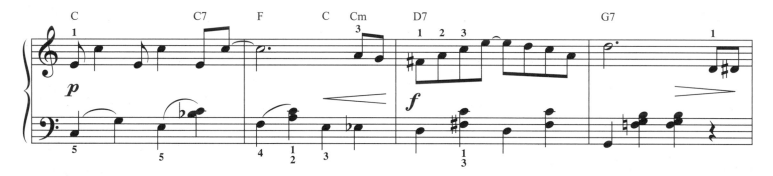

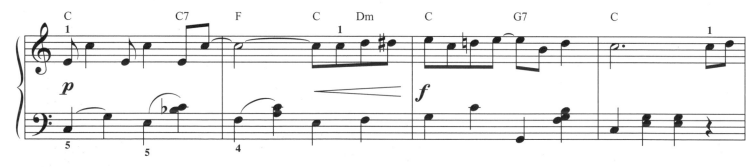

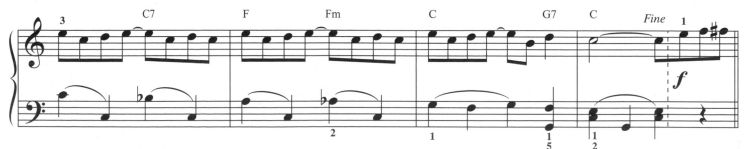

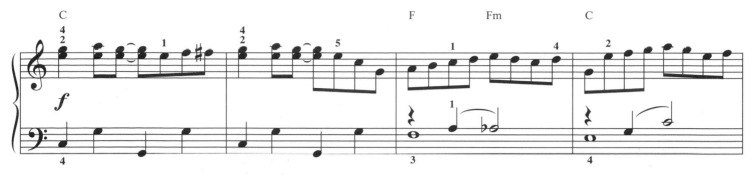

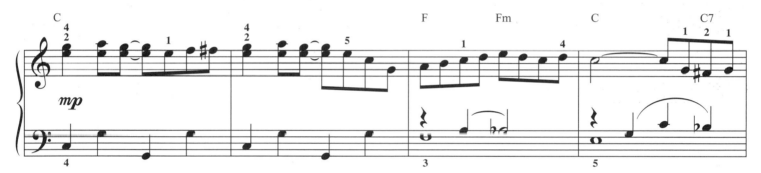

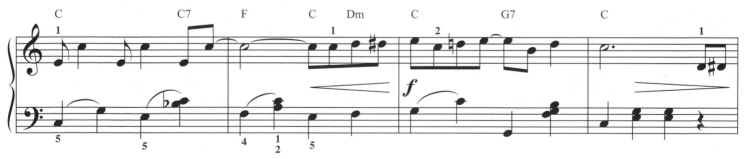

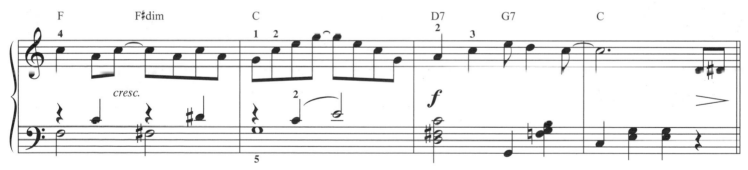

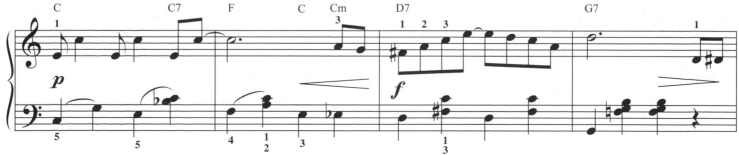

40

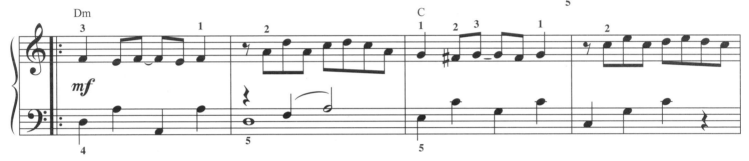

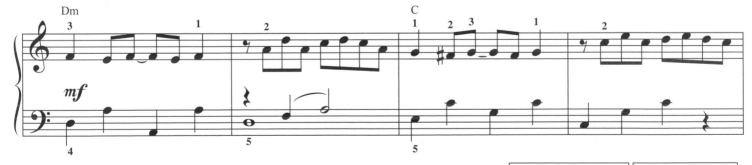

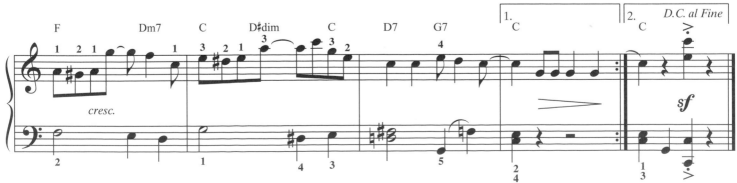

Rumba Revels
(La Cucaracha)

Lively rumba tempo (♩ = 84)

Denes Agay

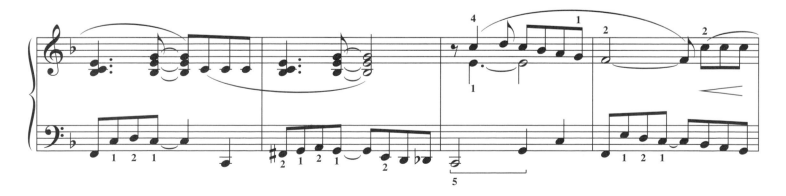

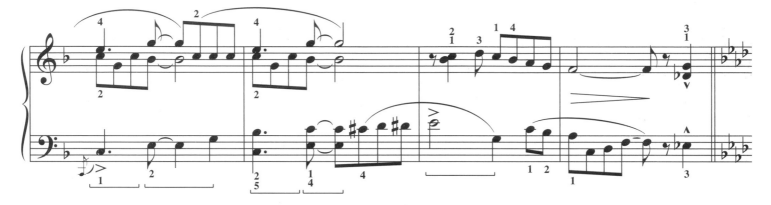

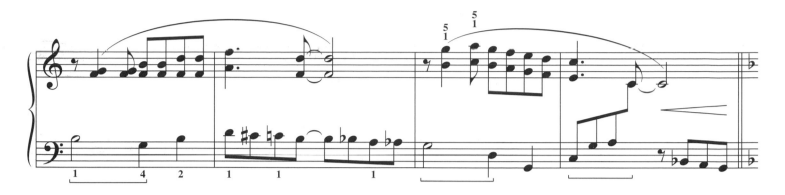

Tango "La Cumparsita"

C.H. Matos Rodriguez

Marked, moderate tempo

Alexander's Ragtime Band

Irving Berlin
(1888–1989)

Come on and hear,⎯ Come on and hear⎯ Al - ex - an - der's Rag time Band.⎯

⎯ Come on the hear,⎯ Come on and hear⎯ It's the best hand in the land.⎯

They can play a bu - gle call like you nev - er heard be - fore,

So nat - ur - al that you want to go to war; That's just the best - est band what

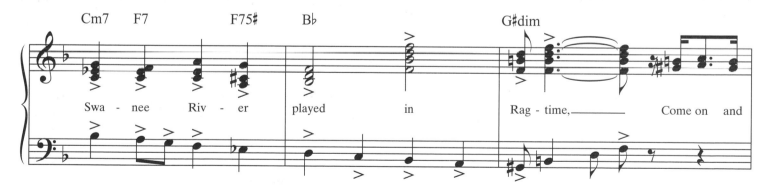

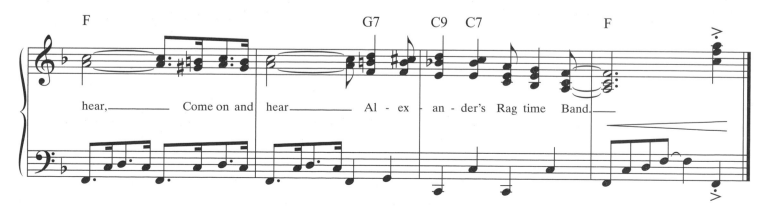

Nola

Felix Arndt

Light "Soft - Shoe" Beat

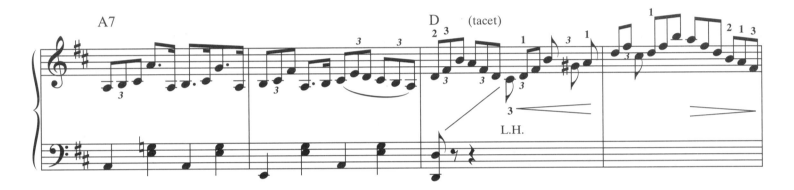

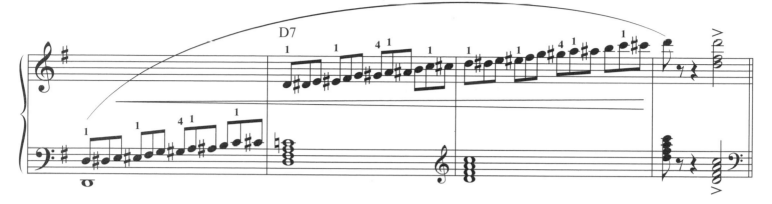

Boogie-Woogie
("Short'nin' Bread")

Denes Agay

Waltz from "Der Rosenkavalier"

Richard Strauss
(1864–1949)

Rather slow

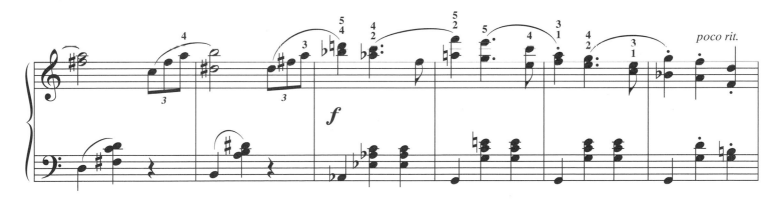

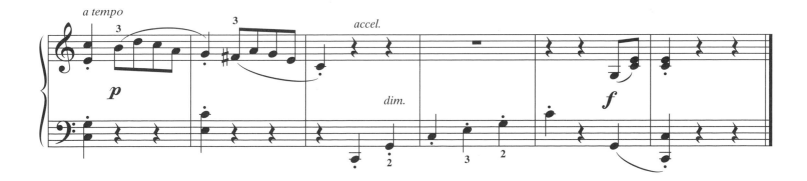

J.D.'s Boogie-Woogie

Jimmy Dorsey and
Marvin "Lefty" Wright

Moderate boogie tempo

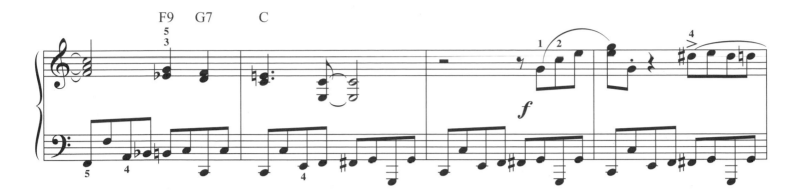

Square Dance

Traditional

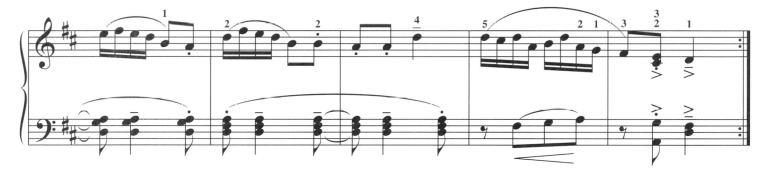

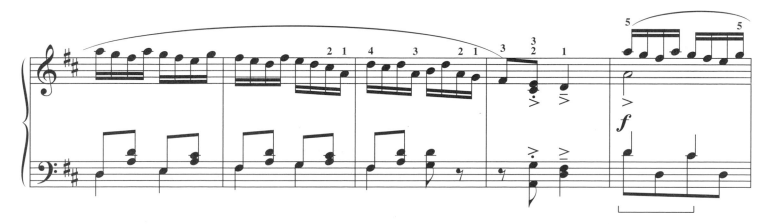

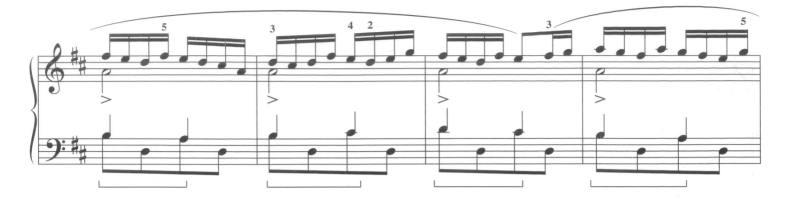

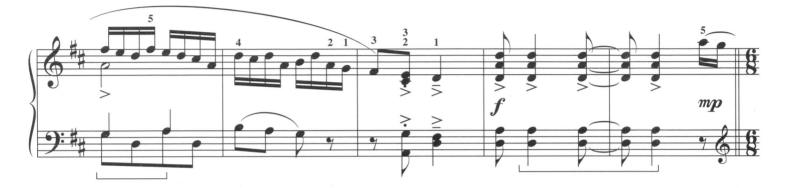

Irish Washerwoman
Allegro

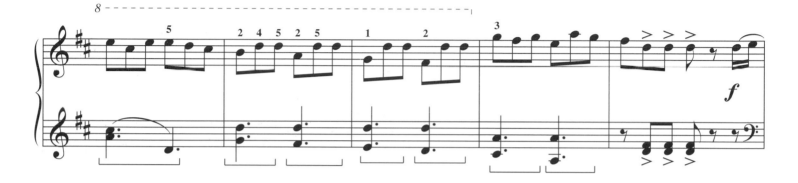

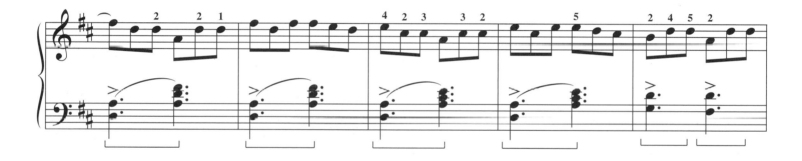

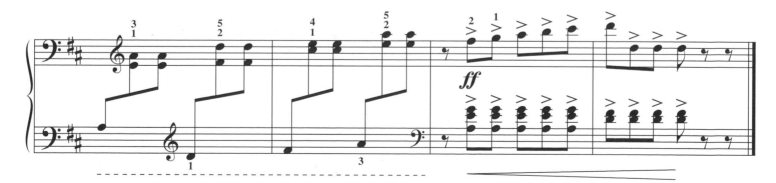

Clarinet Polka

Rev. by Denes Agay
(1911–)

Bright polka tempo

Trio

Charleston

Cecil Mack and
Jimmy Johnson

Lively, strong beat

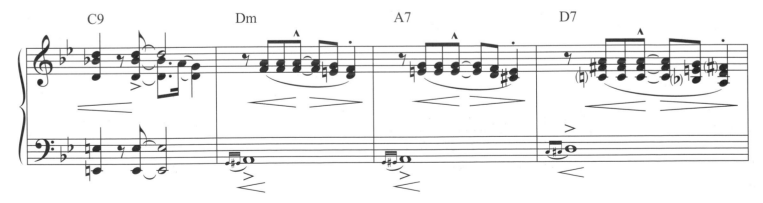

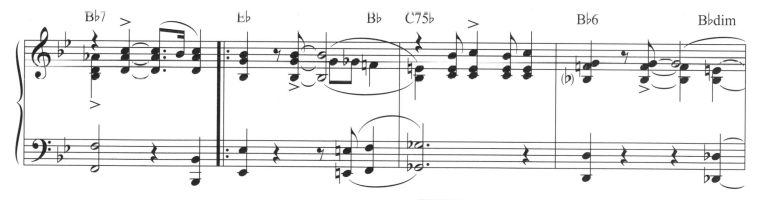

Palm Garden
(Slow Blues)

Thomas "Fats" Waller
(1904–1943)

Slow blues tempo

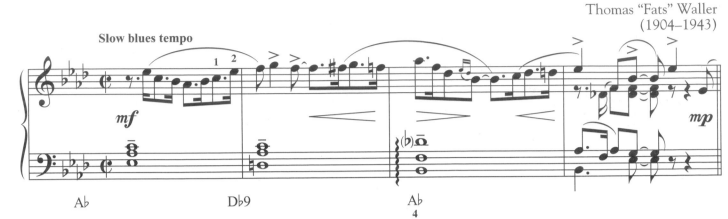

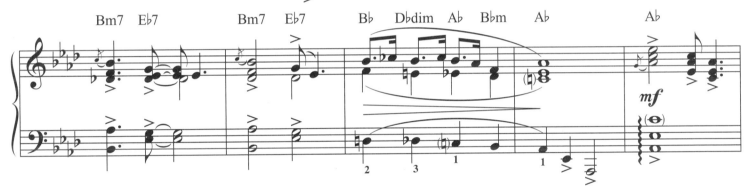

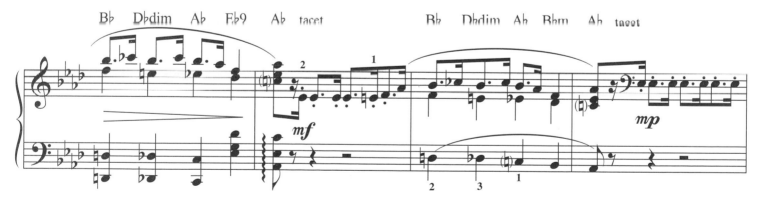

Mardi Gras Bolero

Denes Agay

Quite lively (♩ = ca 100)

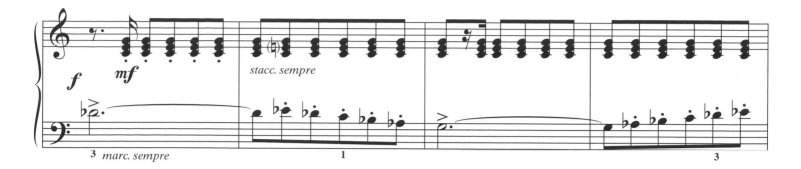

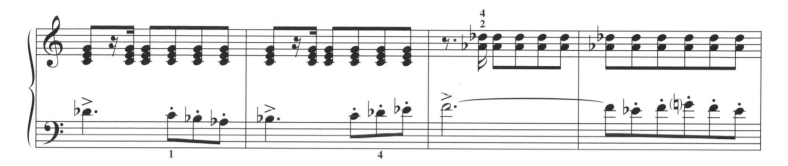

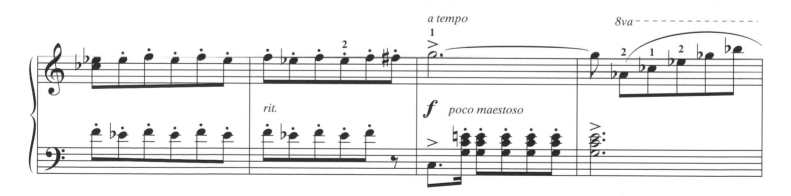

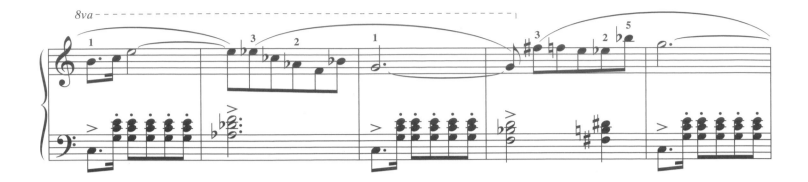

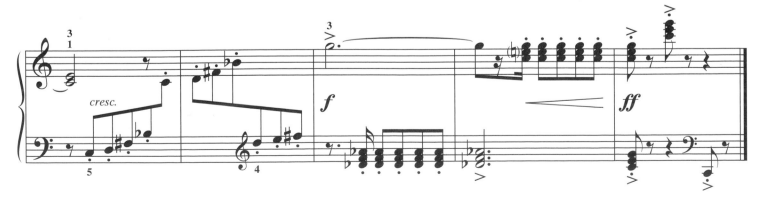

Hava Nagila

Traditional Israeli Folk Dance

Bright tempo

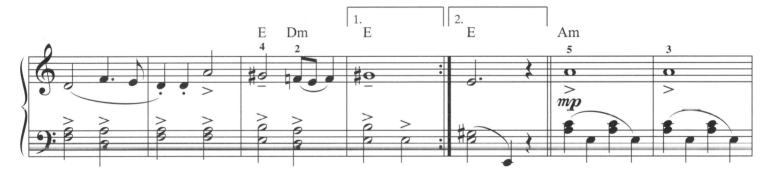

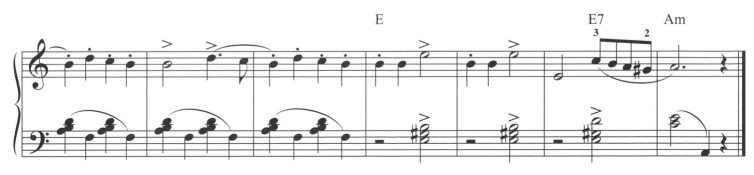

Tuxedo Junction
(Swing)

Buddy Feyne, Erskine Hawkins,
William Johnson and Julian Dash

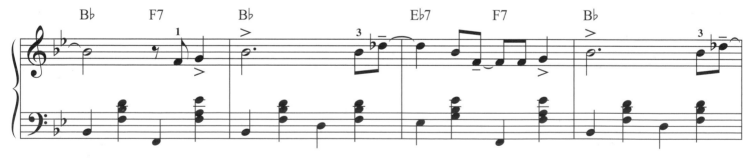

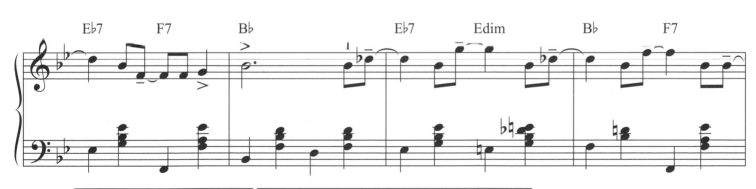

Dizzy's Dilemma

Charlie Shavers
(1917–1971)

Moderately bright swing

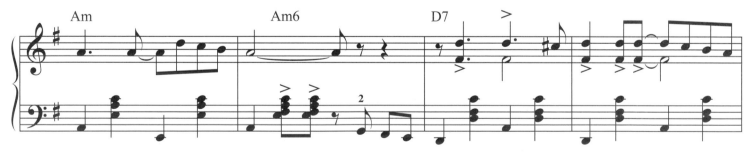

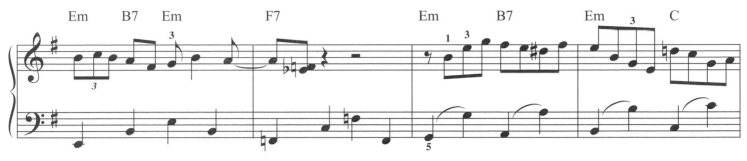

Blowin' Hot and Cool

Gerald Martin

Moderately fast

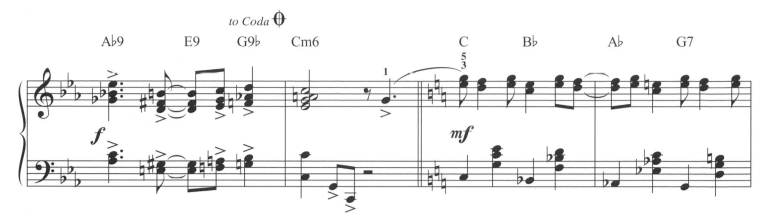

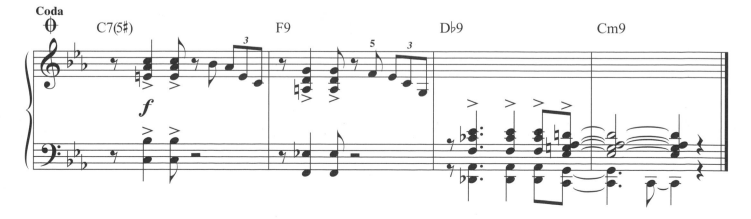

Another Shade of Blue

Denes Agay

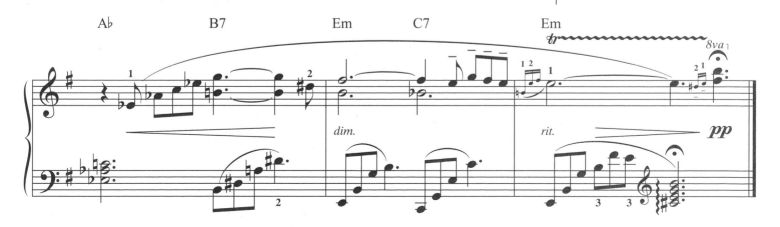

The Happy Organ
(Rock)

Ken Wood, David Clowney
and James J. Kriegsmann

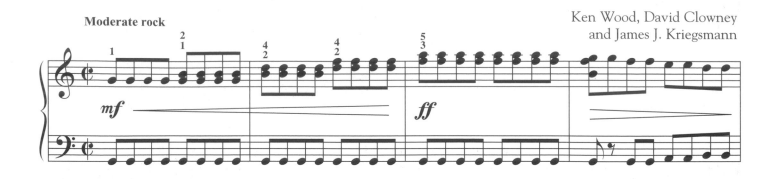

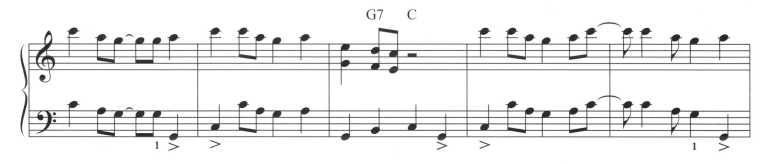

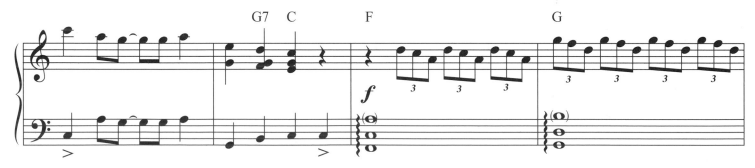

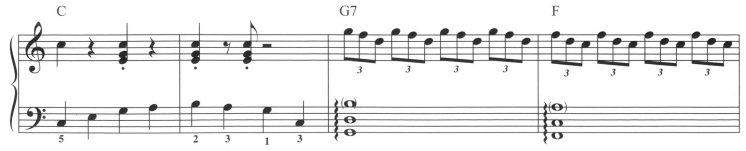

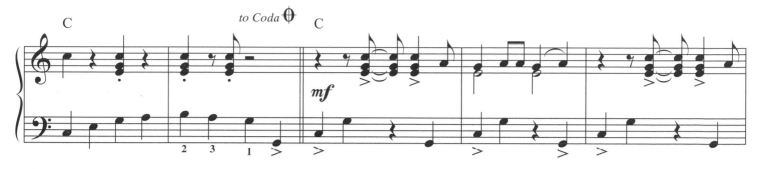

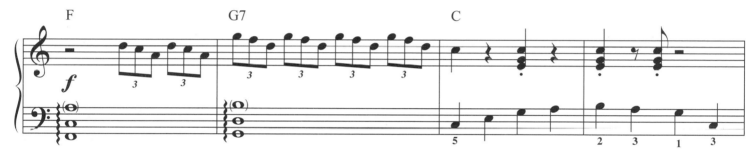

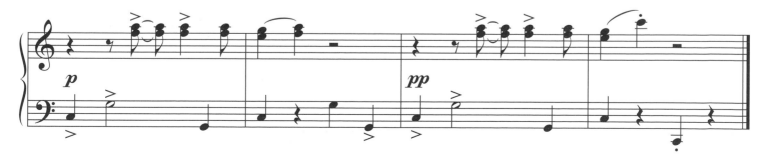

Smoky on the Rocks

Gerald Martin

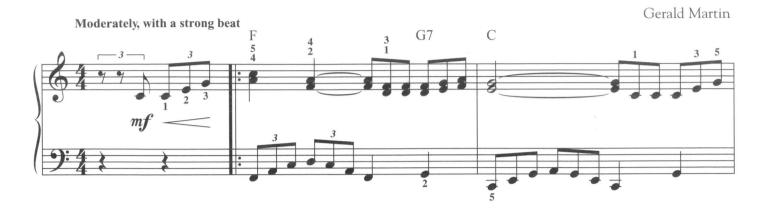

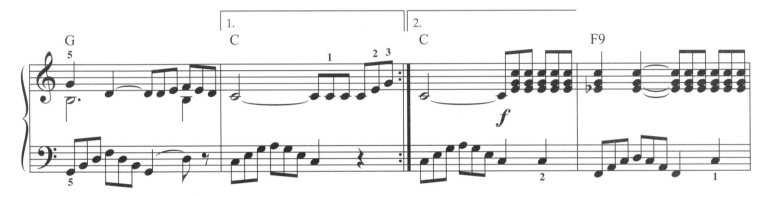

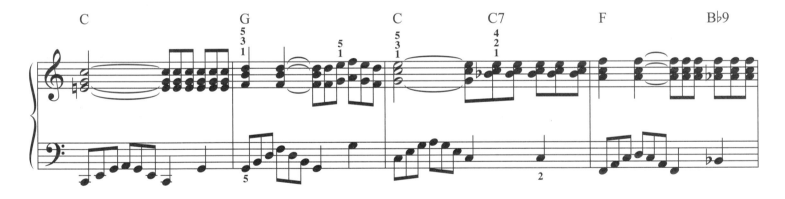